Fertility Awareness NFP Charts

Sympto-Thermal Method

The charts provided in this book are intended for personal use for those who have been trained in the use of fertility awareness and natural family planning methods by a certified instructor. See the list of resources in the back of this chart book to learn more about how to chart using the Sympto-Thermal Method.

You agree to indemnify, defend, and hold harmless the authors of these charts from any liability, loss, claim, and expense related to your use of these charts. Your use of these charts shall constitute your acceptance of these terms.

ISBN 979-8-4606-1181-2

Sympto-Thermal Method NFP Chart

Cycle Start Date: 08 / 16 / 2021

Achieve ☐   X Avoid

Cycle Day	1	2	3	4	5	6	7	8	9	10	11	12	13	14	15	16	17	18	19	20	21	22	23	24	25	26	27	28	29	30	31	32	33	34	35	36	37	38	39	40
Date	16	17	18	19	20	21	22	23	24	25	26	27	28	29	30	31	1	2	3	4	5	6	7	8	9	10	11	12	13	14	15	16	17							
Day of Week	M	T	W	Th	F	S	S	M	T	W	Th	F	S	S	M	T	W	Th	F	S	S	M	T	W	Th	F	S	S	M	T	W	Th	F							
Time	8:00						10:00		8:00							9:30	8:00			9:00	8:00																			

Basal Body Temperature (°F)

°C: 37.9 37.8 37.7 37.6 37.5 37.4 37.3 37.2 37.1 37.0 36.9 36.8 36.7 36.6 36.5 36.4 36.3 36.2 36.1 36.0 35.9

EXAMPLE

	Fertility		Menstruation		Mucus	Sensation	Cervix	Intercourse

*This is just one example of a standard cycle to demonstrate how this chart is used. Variations in cycles can occur (long and short cycles, early ovulation, etc.). Please see the resource list at the back of this book to learn more.

Notes:

Example:

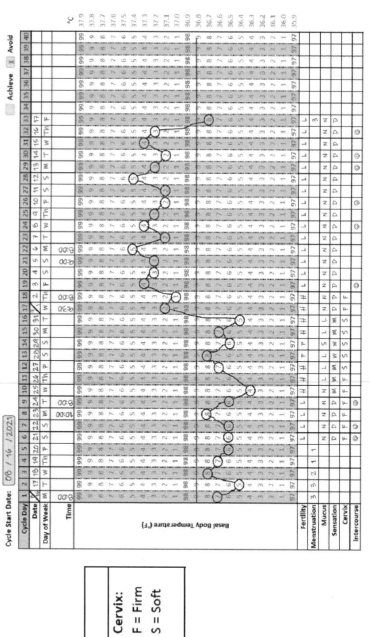

Key

Fertility:	Menstruation:	Mucus:	Sensation:	Cervix:
L = Low	1 = Light	N = Nothing	D = Dry	F = Firm
H = High	2 = Moderate	L = Little	M = Moist	S = Soft
P = Peak	3 = Heavy	S = Sticky	W = Wet	

Sympto-Thermal Method NFP Chart

Cycle Start Date: ___ / ___ / ___

☐ Achieve ☐ Avoid

Cycle Day	1	2	3	4	5	6	7	8	9	10	11	12	13	14	15	16	17	18	19	20	21	22	23	24	25	26	27	28	29	30	31	32	33	34	35	36	37	38	39	40
Date																																								
Day of Week																																								
Time																																								

°C (column): 37.9, 37.8, 37.7, 37.6, 37.5, 37.4, 37.3, 37.2, 37.1, 37.0, 36.9, 36.8, 36.7, 36.6, 36.5, 36.4, 36.3, 36.2, 36.1, 36.0, 35.9

Basal Body Temperature (°F): 99 9 8 7 6 5 4 3 2 1 98 9 8 7 6 5 4 3 2 1 97

Fertility																																								
Menstruation																																								
Mucus																																								
Sensation																																								
Cervix																																								
Intercourse																																								

Notes:

Example:

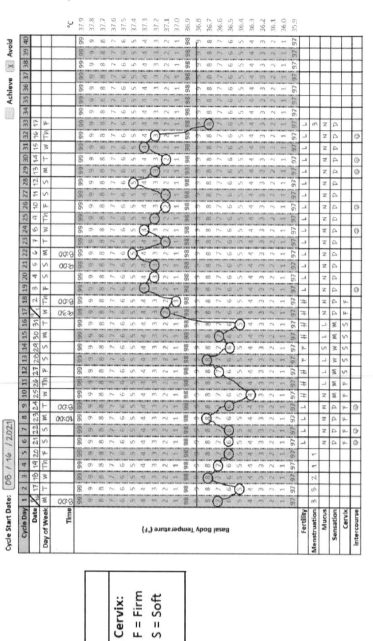

Key

Fertility:	Menstruation:	Mucus:	Sensation:	Cervix:
L = Low	1 = Light	N = Nothing	D = Dry	F = Firm
H = High	2 = Moderate	L = Little	M = Moist	S = Soft
P = Peak	3 = Heavy	S = Sticky	W = Wet	

Sympto-Thermal Method NFP Chart

Cycle Start Date: ___ / ___ / ___

Achieve ☐   Avoid ☐

Cycle Day	1	2	3	4	5	6	7	8	9	10	11	12	13	14	15	16	17	18	19	20	21	22	23	24	25	26	27	28	29	30	31	32	33	34	35	36	37	38	39	40
Date																																								
Day of Week																																								
Time																																								

Basal Body Temperature (°F) — with °C scale:

°C	°F
37.9	99.9
37.8	99.8
37.7	99.7
37.6	99.6
37.5	99.5
37.4	99.4
37.3	99.3
37.2	99.2
37.1	99.1
37.0	99.0
36.9	98.9
36.8	98.8
36.7	98.7
36.6	98.6
36.5	98.5
36.4	98.4
36.3	98.3
36.2	98.2
36.1	98.1
36.0	98.0
35.9	97.9

Fertility

Menstruation

Mucus

Sensation

Cervix

Intercourse

Notes:

Example:

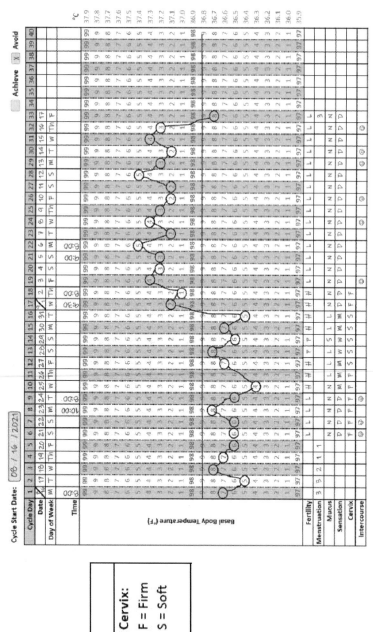

Key

Fertility:	Menstruation:	Mucus:	Sensation:	Cervix:
L = Low	1 = Light	N = Nothing	D = Dry	F = Firm
H = High	2 = Moderate	L = Little	M = Moist	S = Soft
P = Peak	3 = Heavy	S = Sticky	W = Wet	

Sympto-Thermal Method NFP Chart

Cycle Start Date: ___ / ___ / ___

Achieve ☐   Avoid ☐

Cycle Day	1	2	3	4	5	6	7	8	9	10	11	12	13	14	15	16	17	18	19	20	21	22	23	24	25	26	27	28	29	30	31	32	33	34	35	36	37	38	39	40	°C
Date																																									
Day of Week																																									
Time																																									

Basal Body Temperature (°F) — grid rows: 99, 9, 8, 7, 6, 5, 4, 3, 2, 1, 98, 9, 8, 7, 6, 5, 4, 3, 2, 1, 97

°C scale: 37.9, 37.8, 37.7, 37.6, 37.5, 37.4, 37.3, 37.2, 37.1, 37.0, 36.9, 36.8, 36.7, 36.6, 36.5, 36.4, 36.3, 36.2, 36.1, 36.0, 35.9

Fertility																																									
Menstruation																																									
Mucus																																									
Sensation																																									
Cervix																																									
Intercourse																																									

Notes:

Example:

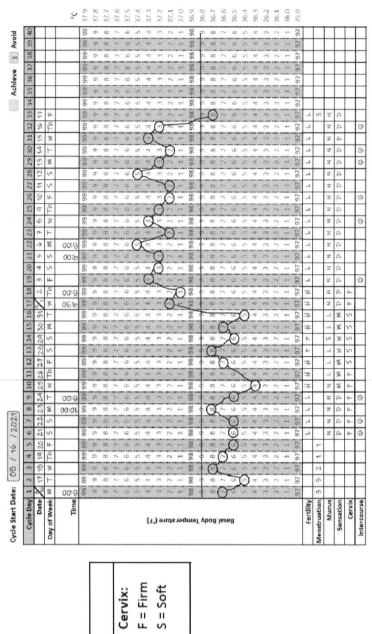

Key

Fertility:	Menstruation:	Mucus:	Sensation:	Cervix:
L = Low	1 = Light	N = Nothing	D = Dry	F = Firm
H = High	2 = Moderate	L = Little	M = Moist	S = Soft
P = Peak	3 = Heavy	S = Sticky	W = Wet	

Sympto-Thermal Method NFP Chart

Cycle Start Date: ___ / ___ / ___

Achieve ☐   Avoid ☐

Cycle Day	1	2	3	4	5	6	7	8	9	10	11	12	13	14	15	16	17	18	19	20	21	22	23	24	25	26	27	28	29	30	31	32	33	34	35	36	37	38	39	40
Date																																								
Day of Week																																								
Time																																								

Basal Body Temperature (°F) — °C scale: 37.9, 37.8, 37.7, 37.6, 37.5, 37.4, 37.3, 37.2, 37.1, 37.0, 36.9, 36.8, 36.7, 36.6, 36.5, 36.4, 36.3, 36.2, 36.1, 36.0, 35.9

Fertility																																								
Menstruation																																								
Mucus																																								
Sensation																																								
Cervix																																								
Intercourse																																								

Notes:

Example:

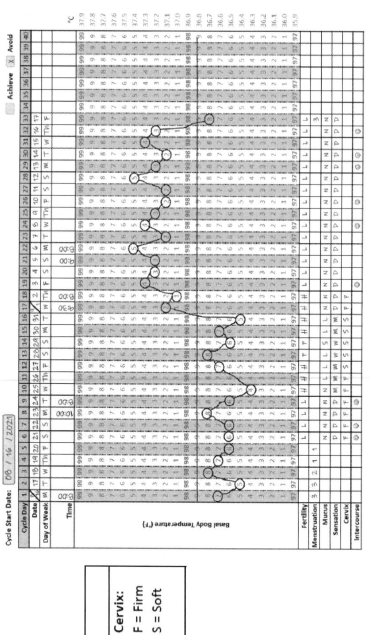

Key

Fertility:	Menstruation:	Mucus:	Sensation:	Cervix:
L = Low	1 = Light	N = Nothing	D = Dry	F = Firm
H = High	2 = Moderate	L = Little	M = Moist	S = Soft
P = Peak	3 = Heavy	S = Sticky	W = Wet	

Sympto-Thermal Method NFP Chart

Cycle Start Date: ___ / ___ / ___

Achieve ▢   Avoid ▢

Cycle Day	1	2	3	4	5	6	7	8	9	10	11	12	13	14	15	16	17	18	19	20	21	22	23	24	25	26	27	28	29	30	31	32	33	34	35	36	37	38	39	40	°C
Date																																									
Day of Week																																									
Time																																									

Basal Body Temperature (°F) — rows from 99 down to 97 corresponding to °C scale:
37.9, 37.8, 37.7, 37.6, 37.5, 37.4, 37.3, 37.2, 37.1, 37.0, 36.9, 36.8, 36.7, 36.6, 36.5, 36.4, 36.3, 36.2, 36.1, 36.0, 35.9

| Fertility |
| Menstruation |
| Mucus |
| Sensation |
| Cervix |
| Intercourse |

Notes:

Example:

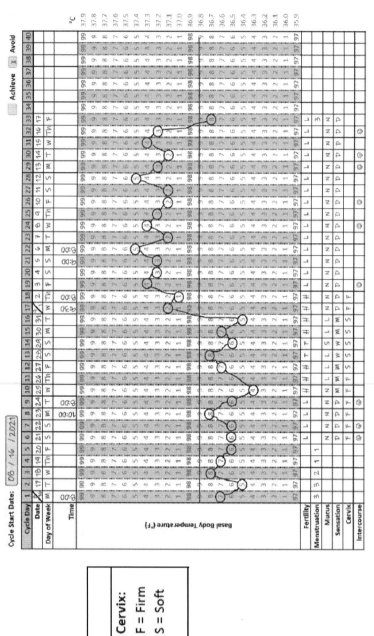

Key			
Fertility:	**Menstruation:**	**Mucus:**	**Sensation:**	**Cervix:**
L = Low	1 = Light	N = Nothing	D = Dry	F = Firm
H = High	2 = Moderate	L = Little	M = Moist	S = Soft
P = Peak	3 = Heavy	S = Sticky	W = Wet	

Sympto-Thermal Method NFP Chart

Cycle Start Date: ___ / ___ / ___

Achieve ☐   Avoid ☐

Cycle Day	1	2	3	4	5	6	7	8	9	10	11	12	13	14	15	16	17	18	19	20	21	22	23	24	25	26	27	28	29	30	31	32	33	34	35	36	37	38	39	40
Date																																								
Day of Week																																								
Time																																								

Basal Body Temperature (°F) — °C scale: 37.9, 37.8, 37.7, 37.6, 37.5, 37.4, 37.3, 37.2, 37.1, 37.0, 36.9, 36.8, 36.7, 36.6, 36.5, 36.4, 36.3, 36.2, 36.1, 36.0, 35.9

(Temperature grid rows: 99, 9, 8, 7, 6, 5, 4, 3, 2, 1, 98, 9, 8, 7, 6, 5, 4, 3, 2, 1, 97)

Fertility	
Menstruation	
Mucus	
Sensation	
Cervix	
Intercourse	

Notes:

Example:

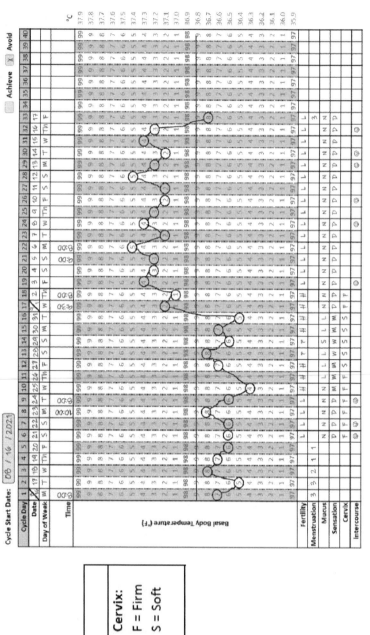

Cycle Start Date: 08 / 16 / 2021

Achieve	X	Avoid

Key

Fertility:	Menstruation:	Mucus:	Sensation:	Cervix:
L = Low	1 = Light	N = Nothing	D = Dry	F = Firm
H = High	2 = Moderate	L = Little	M = Moist	S = Soft
P = Peak	3 = Heavy	S = Sticky	W = Wet	

Sympto-Thermal Method NFP Chart

Cycle Start Date: / /

Achieve   Avoid

Cycle Day	1	2	3	4	5	6	7	8	9	10	11	12	13	14	15	16	17	18	19	20	21	22	23	24	25	26	27	28	29	30	31	32	33	34	35	36	37	38	39	40
Date																																								
Day of Week																																								
Time																																								

Basal Body Temperature (°F) / °C scale: 37.9, 37.8, 37.7, 37.6, 37.5, 37.4, 37.3, 37.2, 37.1, 37.0, 36.9, 36.8, 36.7, 36.6, 36.5, 36.4, 36.3, 36.2, 36.1, 36.0, 35.9

Temperature grid values (°F, top to bottom): 99, 9, 8, 7, 6, 5, 4, 3, 2, 1, 98, 9, 8, 7, 6, 5, 4, 3, 2, 1, 97

Fertility																																								
Menstruation																																								
Mucus																																								
Sensation																																								
Cervix																																								
Intercourse																																								

Notes:

Example:

Cycle Start Date: 08 / 16 / 2021

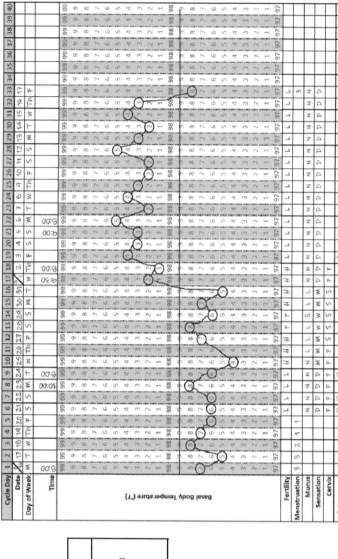

Key

Fertility:	Menstruation:	Mucus:	Sensation:	Cervix:
L = Low	1 = Light	N = Nothing	D = Dry	F = Firm
H = High	2 = Moderate	L = Little	M = Moist	S = Soft
P = Peak	3 = Heavy	S = Sticky	W = Wet	

Sympto-Thermal Method NFP Chart

Cycle Start Date: ___ / ___ / ___

Achieve Avoid

Cycle Day	1	2	3	4	5	6	7	8	9	10	11	12	13	14	15	16	17	18	19	20	21	22	23	24	25	26	27	28	29	30	31	32	33	34	35	36	37	38	39	40
Date																																								
Day of Week																																								
Time																																								

Basal Body Temperature (°F) / °C

°C	
37.9	99
37.8	9
37.7	8
37.6	7
37.5	6
37.4	5
37.3	4
37.2	3
37.1	2
37.0	1
36.9	98
36.8	9
36.7	8
36.6	7
36.5	6
36.4	5
36.3	4
36.2	3
36.1	2
36.0	1
35.9	97

Fertility																																								
Menstruation																																								
Mucus																																								
Sensation																																								
Cervix																																								
Intercourse																																								

Notes:

Example:

Cycle Start Date: 08 / 16 / 2021

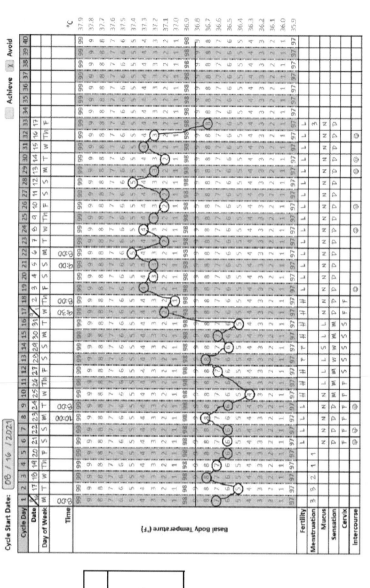

Key

Fertility:	Menstruation:	Mucus:	Sensation:	Cervix:
L = Low	1 = Light	N = Nothing	D = Dry	F = Firm
H = High	2 = Moderate	L = Little	M = Moist	S = Soft
P = Peak	3 = Heavy	S = Sticky	W = Wet	

Sympto-Thermal Method NFP Chart

Cycle Start Date: ___ / ___ / ___

Achieve Avoid

Cycle Day	1	2	3	4	5	6	7	8	9	10	11	12	13	14	15	16	17	18	19	20	21	22	23	24	25	26	27	28	29	30	31	32	33	34	35	36	37	38	39	40
Date																																								
Day of Week																																								
Time																																								

Basal Body Temperature (°F) / °C scale: 37.9, 37.8, 37.7, 37.6, 37.5, 37.4, 37.3, 37.2, 37.1, 37.0, 36.9, 36.8, 36.7, 36.6, 36.5, 36.4, 36.3, 36.2, 36.1, 36.0, 35.9

(Temperature grid values: 99, 9, 8, 7, 6, 5, 4, 3, 2, 1, 98, 9, 8, 7, 6, 5, 4, 3, 2, 1, 97)

Fertility																																								
Menstruation																																								
Mucus																																								
Sensation																																								
Cervix																																								
Intercourse																																								

Notes:

Example:

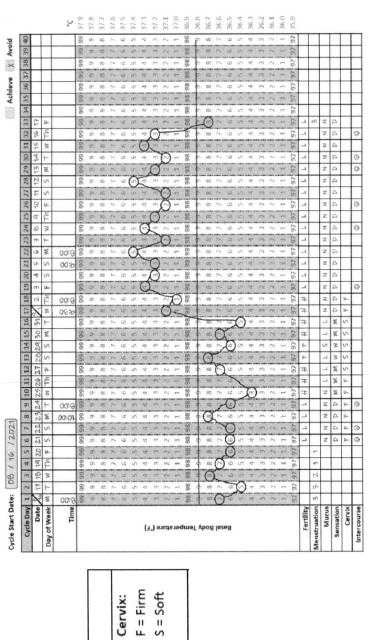

Cycle Start Date: 08 / 16 / 2021

Key

Fertility:	Menstruation:	Mucus:	Sensation:	Cervix:
L = Low	1 = Light	N = Nothing	D = Dry	F = Firm
H = High	2 = Moderate	L = Little	M = Moist	S = Soft
P = Peak	3 = Heavy	S = Sticky	W = Wet	

Sympto-Thermal Method NFP Chart

Cycle Start Date: ___ / ___ / ___

Achieve ☐   Avoid ☐

Cycle Day	1	2	3	4	5	6	7	8	9	10	11	12	13	14	15	16	17	18	19	20	21	22	23	24	25	26	27	28	29	30	31	32	33	34	35	36	37	38	39	40
Date																																								
Day of Week																																								
Time																																								

Basal Body Temperature (°F) / °C scale:
37.9, 37.8, 37.7, 37.6, 37.5, 37.4, 37.3, 37.2, 37.1, 37.0, 36.9, 36.8, 36.7, 36.6, 36.5, 36.4, 36.3, 36.2, 36.1, 36.0, 35.9

Fertility
Menstruation
Mucus
Sensation
Cervix
Intercourse

Notes:

Example:

Cycle Start Date: 08 / 16 / 2021

	Fertility	Menstruation	Mucus	Sensation	Cervix	Intercourse

Key

Fertility:	Menstruation:	Mucus:	Sensation:	Cervix:
L = Low	1 = Light	N = Nothing	D = Dry	F = Firm
H = High	2 = Moderate	L = Little	M = Moist	S = Soft
P = Peak	3 = Heavy	S = Sticky	W = Wet	

Sympto-Thermal Method NFP Chart

Cycle Start Date: ___ / ___ / ___

Achieve ☐ Avoid ☐

Cycle Day	1	2	3	4	5	6	7	8	9	10	11	12	13	14	15	16	17	18	19	20	21	22	23	24	25	26	27	28	29	30	31	32	33	34	35	36	37	38	39	40	°C
Date																																									
Day of Week																																									
Time																																									

Basal Body Temperature (°F)

																																									°C
99																																									37.9
9																																									37.8
8																																									37.7
7																																									37.6
6																																									37.5
5																																									37.4
4																																									37.3
3																																									37.2
2																																									37.1
1																																									37.0
98																																									36.9
9																																									36.8
8																																									36.7
7																																									36.6
6																																									36.5
5																																									36.4
4																																									36.3
3																																									36.2
2																																									36.1
1																																									36.0
97																																									35.9

Fertility																																								
Menstruation																																								
Mucus																																								
Sensation																																								
Cervix																																								
Intercourse																																								

Notes:

Example:

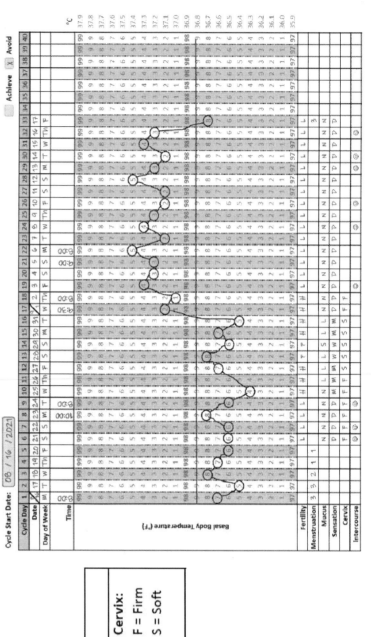

Key

Fertility:	Menstruation:	Mucus:	Sensation:	Cervix:
L = Low	1 = Light	N = Nothing	D = Dry	F = Firm
H = High	2 = Moderate	L = Little	M = Moist	S = Soft
P = Peak	3 = Heavy	S = Sticky	W = Wet	

Sympto-Thermal Method NFP Chart

Cycle Start Date: ___ / ___ / ___

Achieve ☐ Avoid ☐

Cycle Day	1	2	3	4	5	6	7	8	9	10	11	12	13	14	15	16	17	18	19	20	21	22	23	24	25	26	27	28	29	30	31	32	33	34	35	36	37	38	39	40
Date																																								
Day of Week																																								
Time																																								

°C temperature scale (right axis): 37.9, 37.8, 37.7, 37.6, 37.5, 37.4, 37.3, 37.2, 37.1, 37.0, 36.9, 36.8, 36.7, 36.6, 36.5, 36.4, 36.3, 36.2, 36.1, 36.0, 35.9

Basal Body Temperature (°F)

| Fertility |
| Menstruation |
| Mucus |
| Sensation |
| Cervix |
| Intercourse |

Notes:

Example:

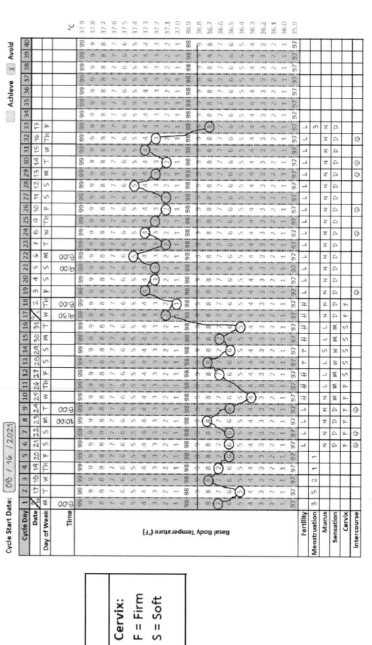

Key

Fertility:	Menstruation:	Mucus:	Sensation:	Cervix:
L = Low	1 = Light	N = Nothing	D = Dry	F = Firm
H = High	2 = Moderate	L = Little	M = Moist	S = Soft
P = Peak	3 = Heavy	S = Sticky	W = Wet	

Sympto-Thermal Method NFP Chart

Cycle Start Date: ___ / ___ / ___

Achieve ☐   Avoid ☐

Cycle Day	1	2	3	4	5	6	7	8	9	10	11	12	13	14	15	16	17	18	19	20	21	22	23	24	25	26	27	28	29	30	31	32	33	34	35	36	37	38	39	40
Date																																								
Day of Week																																								
Time																																								

Basal Body Temperature (°F) — scale in °C: 37.9, 37.8, 37.7, 37.6, 37.5, 37.4, 37.3, 37.2, 37.1, 37.0, 36.9, 36.8, 36.7, 36.6, 36.5, 36.4, 36.3, 36.2, 36.1, 36.0, 35.9

Fertility	
Menstruation	
Mucus	
Sensation	
Cervix	
Intercourse	

Notes:

Example:

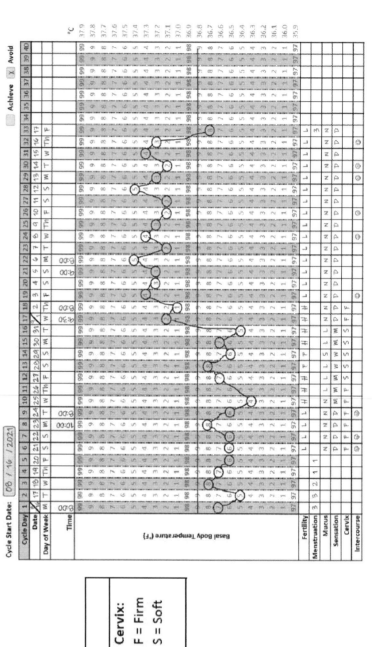

Cycle Start Date: 08 / 16 / 2021

Key

Fertility:	Menstruation:	Mucus:	Sensation:	Cervix:
L = Low	1 = Light	N = Nothing	D = Dry	F = Firm
H = High	2 = Moderate	L = Little	M = Moist	S = Soft
P = Peak	3 = Heavy	S = Sticky	W = Wet	

Sympto-Thermal Method NFP Chart

Cycle Start Date: ___ / ___ / ___

Achieve ☐ Avoid ☐

Cycle Day	1	2	3	4	5	6	7	8	9	10	11	12	13	14	15	16	17	18	19	20	21	22	23	24	25	26	27	28	29	30	31	32	33	34	35	36	37	38	39	40	°C
Date																																									
Day of Week																																									
Time																																									

Basal Body Temperature (°F) — rows from 99.9 (37.9 °C) down to 97 (35.9 °C)

°F scale	°C
99	37.9
9	37.8
8	37.7
7	37.6
6	37.5
5	37.4
4	37.3
3	37.2
2	37.1
1	37.0
98	36.9
9	36.8
8	36.7
7	36.6
6	36.5
5	36.4
4	36.3
3	36.2
2	36.1
1	36.0
97	35.9

Fertility																																									
Menstruation																																									
Mucus																																									
Sensation																																									
Cervix																																									
Intercourse																																									

Notes:

Example:

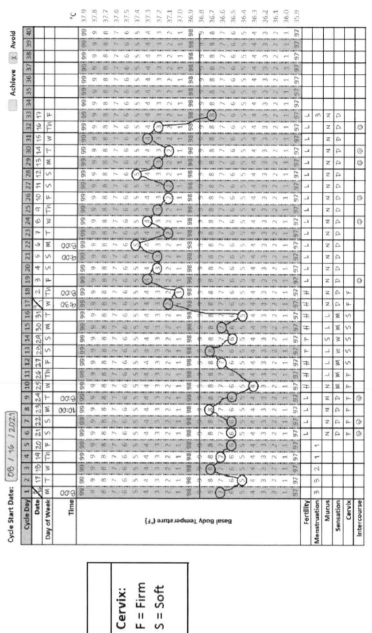

Key

Fertility:	Menstruation:	Mucus:	Sensation:	Cervix:
L = Low	1 = Light	N = Nothing	D = Dry	F = Firm
H = High	2 = Moderate	L = Little	M = Moist	S = Soft
P = Peak	3 = Heavy	S = Sticky	W = Wet	

Sympto-Thermal Method NFP Chart

Cycle Start Date: ___ / ___ / ___

Achieve ☐   Avoid ☐

Cycle Day	1	2	3	4	5	6	7	8	9	10	11	12	13	14	15	16	17	18	19	20	21	22	23	24	25	26	27	28	29	30	31	32	33	34	35	36	37	38	39	40	°C
Date																																									
Day of Week																																									
Time																																									

Basal Body Temperature (°F)

Temperature scale (top to bottom): 99.9/37.9, 99.9/37.8, 99.8/37.7, 99.7/37.6, 99.6/37.5, 99.5/37.4, 99.4/37.3, 99.3/37.2, 99.2/37.1, 99.1/37.0, 98.9/36.9, 98.8/36.8, 98.7/36.7, 98.6/36.6, 98.5/36.5, 98.4/36.4, 98.3/36.3, 98.2/36.2, 98.1/36.1, 98.0/36.0, 97.9/35.9

Fertility																																									
Menstruation																																									
Mucus																																									
Sensation																																									
Cervix																																									
Intercourse																																									

Notes:

Example:

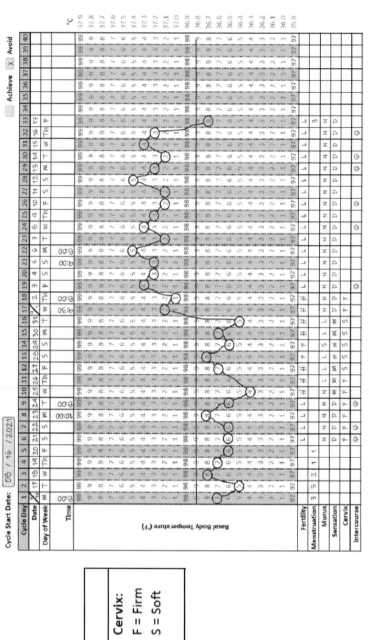

Key

Fertility:	Menstruation:	Mucus:	Sensation:	Cervix:
L = Low	1 = Light	N = Nothing	D = Dry	F = Firm
H = High	2 = Moderate	L = Little	M = Moist	S = Soft
P = Peak	3 = Heavy	S = Sticky	W = Wet	

Sympto-Thermal Method NFP Chart

Cycle Start Date: ___ / ___ / ___

Achieve ▢   Avoid ▢

Cycle Day	1	2	3	4	5	6	7	8	9	10	11	12	13	14	15	16	17	18	19	20	21	22	23	24	25	26	27	28	29	30	31	32	33	34	35	36	37	38	39	40
Date																																								
Day of Week																																								
Time																																								

Basal Body Temperature (°F) / °C scale: 37.9, 37.8, 37.7, 37.6, 37.5, 37.4, 37.3, 37.2, 37.1, 37.0, 36.9, 36.8, 36.7, 36.6, 36.5, 36.4, 36.3, 36.2, 36.1, 36.0, 35.9

(°F rows: 99, 9, 8, 7, 6, 5, 4, 3, 2, 1, 98, 9, 8, 7, 6, 5, 4, 3, 2, 1, 97)

Fertility																																								
Menstruation																																								
Mucus																																								
Sensation																																								
Cervix																																								
Intercourse																																								

Notes:

Example:

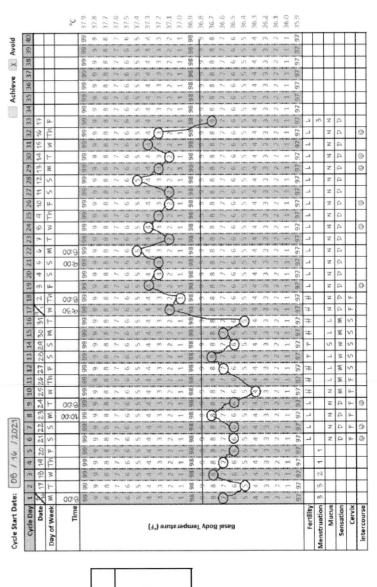

Key

Fertility:	Menstruation:	Mucus:	Sensation:	Cervix:
L = Low	1 = Light	N = Nothing	D = Dry	F = Firm
H = High	2 = Moderate	L = Little	M = Moist	S = Soft
P = Peak	3 = Heavy	S = Sticky	W = Wet	

Sympto-Thermal Method NFP Chart

Cycle Start Date: ___ / ___ / ___

Achieve ☐   Avoid ☐

Cycle Day	1	2	3	4	5	6	7	8	9	10	11	12	13	14	15	16	17	18	19	20	21	22	23	24	25	26	27	28	29	30	31	32	33	34	35	36	37	38	39	40
Date																																								
Day of Week																																								
Time																																								

Basal Body Temperature (°F)

°C scale: 37.9, 37.8, 37.7, 37.6, 37.5, 37.4, 37.3, 37.2, 37.1, 37.0, 36.9, 36.8, 36.7, 36.6, 36.5, 36.4, 36.3, 36.2, 36.1, 36.0, 35.9

°F scale (per column): 99, 9, 8, 7, 6, 5, 4, 3, 2, 1, 98, 9, 8, 7, 6, 5, 4, 3, 2, 1, 97

Fertility																																								
Menstruation																																								
Mucus																																								
Sensation																																								
Cervix																																								
Intercourse																																								

Notes:

Example:

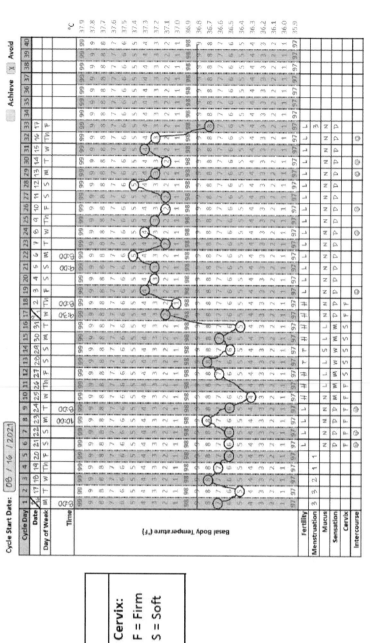

Key

Fertility:	Menstruation:	Mucus:	Sensation:	Cervix:
L = Low	1 = Light	N = Nothing	D = Dry	F = Firm
H = High	2 = Moderate	L = Little	M = Moist	S = Soft
P = Peak	3 = Heavy	S = Sticky	W = Wet	

Sympto-Thermal Method NFP Chart

Cycle Start Date: ___ / ___ / ___

Achieve ▢   Avoid ▢ (shaded)

Cycle Day	1	2	3	4	5	6	7	8	9	10	11	12	13	14	15	16	17	18	19	20	21	22	23	24	25	26	27	28	29	30	31	32	33	34	35	36	37	38	39	40	°C
Date																																									
Day of Week																																									
Time																																									

Basal Body Temperature (°F)

Temperature scale (°C column, top to bottom): 37.9, 37.8, 37.7, 37.6, 37.5, 37.4, 37.3, 37.2, 37.1, 37.0, 36.9, 36.8, 36.7, 36.6, 36.5, 36.4, 36.3, 36.2, 36.1, 36.0, 35.9

Temperature (°F) rows: 99, 9, 8, 7, 6, 5, 4, 3, 2, 1, 98, 9, 8, 7, 6, 5, 4, 3, 2, 1, 97

Fertility	
Menstruation	
Mucus	
Sensation	
Cervix	
Intercourse	

Notes:

Example:

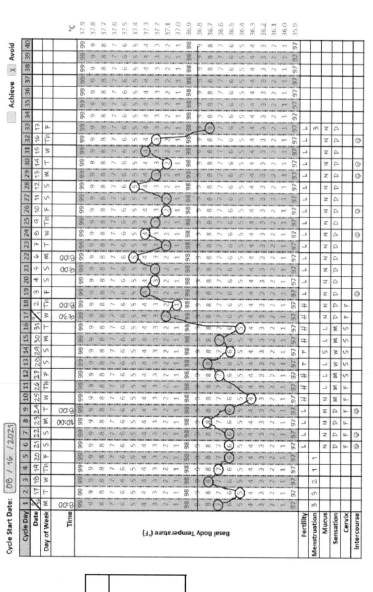

Key

Fertility:	Menstruation:	Mucus:	Sensation:	Cervix:
L = Low	1 = Light	N = Nothing	D = Dry	F = Firm
H = High	2 = Moderate	L = Little	M = Moist	S = Soft
P = Peak	3 = Heavy	S = Sticky	W = Wet	

Sympto-Thermal Method NFP Chart

Cycle Start Date: ___ / ___ / ___

☐ Achieve ☐ Avoid

Cycle Day	1	2	3	4	5	6	7	8	9	10	11	12	13	14	15	16	17	18	19	20	21	22	23	24	25	26	27	28	29	30	31	32	33	34	35	36	37	38	39	40
Date																																								
Day of Week																																								
Time																																								

Basal Body Temperature (°F) — with °C scale: 37.9, 37.8, 37.7, 37.6, 37.5, 37.4, 37.3, 37.2, 37.1, 37.0, 36.9, 36.8, 36.7, 36.6, 36.5, 36.4, 36.3, 36.2, 36.1, 36.0, 35.9

(Temperature grid rows labeled 99, 9, 8, 7, 6, 5, 4, 3, 2, 1, 98, 9, 8, 7, 6, 5, 4, 3, 2, 1, 97)

Fertility	
Menstruation	
Mucus	
Sensation	
Cervix	
Intercourse	

Notes:

Example:

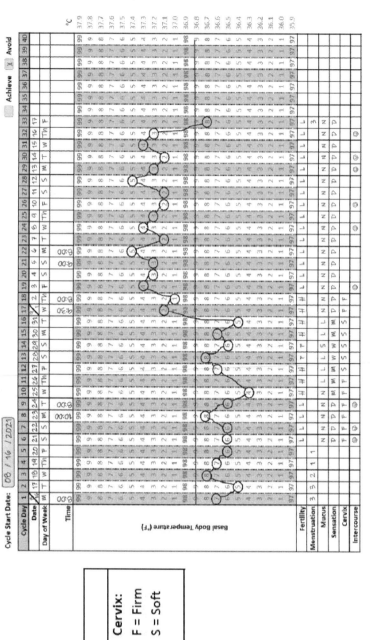

Key

Fertility:	Menstruation:	Mucus:	Sensation:	Cervix:
L = Low	1 = Light	N = Nothing	D = Dry	F = Firm
H = High	2 = Moderate	L = Little	M = Moist	S = Soft
P = Peak	3 = Heavy	S = Sticky	W = Wet	

Sympto-Thermal Method NFP Chart

Cycle Start Date: ___ / ___ / ___

Achieve Avoid

Cycle Day	1	2	3	4	5	6	7	8	9	10	11	12	13	14	15	16	17	18	19	20	21	22	23	24	25	26	27	28	29	30	31	32	33	34	35	36	37	38	39	40	°C
Date																																									
Day of Week																																									
Time																																									

Basal Body Temperature (°F)

Temperature scale (°F / °C): 99 / 37.9, 9 / 37.8, 8 / 37.7, 7 / 37.6, 6 / 37.5, 5 / 37.4, 4 / 37.3, 3 / 37.2, 2 / 37.1, 1 / 37.0, 98 / 36.9, 9 / 36.8, 8 / 36.7, 7 / 36.6, 6 / 36.5, 5 / 36.4, 4 / 36.3, 3 / 36.2, 2 / 36.1, 1 / 36.0, 97 / 35.9

	Fertility
	Menstruation
	Mucus
	Sensation
	Cervix
	Intercourse

Notes:

Example:

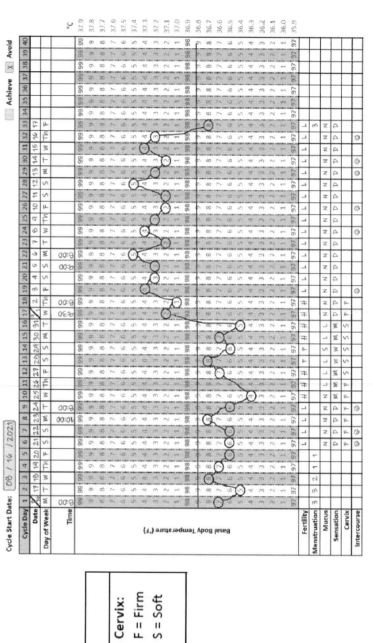

Cycle Start Date: 08 / 16 / 2021

Key

Fertility:	Menstruation:	Mucus:	Sensation:	Cervix:
L = Low	1 = Light	N = Nothing	D = Dry	F = Firm
H = High	2 = Moderate	L = Little	M = Moist	S = Soft
P = Peak	3 = Heavy	S = Sticky	W = Wet	

Sympto-Thermal Method NFP Chart

Cycle Start Date: ___ / ___ / ___

Achieve ▢   Avoid ▨

Cycle Day	1	2	3	4	5	6	7	8	9	10	11	12	13	14	15	16	17	18	19	20	21	22	23	24	25	26	27	28	29	30	31	32	33	34	35	36	37	38	39	40	°C
Date																																									
Day of Week																																									
Time																																									

Basal Body Temperature (°F)

Temperature scale (°F rows with °C equivalents):
99 (37.9), 9 (37.8), 8 (37.7), 7 (37.6), 6 (37.5), 5 (37.4), 4 (37.3), 3 (37.2), 2 (37.1), 1 (37.0), 98 (36.9), 9 (36.8), 8 (36.7), 7 (36.6), 6 (36.5), 5 (36.4), 4 (36.3), 3 (36.2), 2 (36.1), 1 (36.0), 97 (35.9)

	1–40 (Cycle Days)
Fertility	
Menstruation	
Mucus	
Sensation	
Cervix	
Intercourse	

Notes:

Example:

Achieve ☐ Avoid ☒

Cycle Start Date: 08 / 16 / 2021

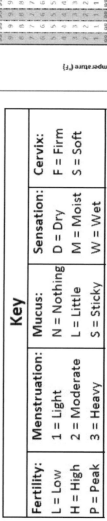

Key

Fertility:	Menstruation:	Mucus:	Sensation:	Cervix:
L = Low	1 = Light	N = Nothing	D = Dry	F = Firm
H = High	2 = Moderate	L = Little	M = Moist	S = Soft
P = Peak	3 = Heavy	S = Sticky	W = Wet	

Sympto-Thermal Method NFP Chart

Cycle Start Date: _____ / _____ / _____

Achieve ☐   Avoid ☐

Cycle Day	°C																			
Date																				
Day of Week																				
Time																				

Basal Body Temperature (°F) — scale from 37.9 °C (99) down to 35.9 °C (97)

°C	°F
37.9	99
37.8	9
37.7	8
37.6	7
37.5	6
37.4	5
37.3	4
37.2	3
37.1	2
37.0	1
36.9	98
36.8	9
36.7	8
36.6	7
36.5	6
36.4	5
36.3	4
36.2	3
36.1	2
36.0	1
35.9	97

Columns numbered 1 – 40 (Cycle Day)

Fertility	
Menstruation	
Mucus	
Sensation	
Cervix	
Intercourse	

Notes:

Example:

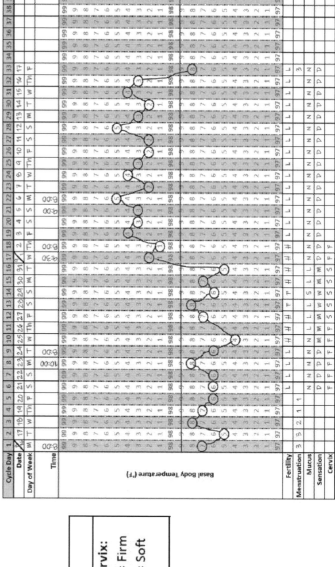

Key

Fertility:	Menstruation:	Mucus:	Sensation:	Cervix:
L = Low	1 = Light	N = Nothing	D = Dry	F = Firm
H = High	2 = Moderate	L = Little	M = Moist	S = Soft
P = Peak	3 = Heavy	S = Sticky	W = Wet	

Sympto-Thermal Method NFP Chart

Cycle Start Date: ___ / ___ / ___

Achieve ▢   Avoid ▢

Cycle Day	1	2	3	4	5	6	7	8	9	10	11	12	13	14	15	16	17	18	19	20	21	22	23	24	25	26	27	28	29	30	31	32	33	34	35	36	37	38	39	40
Date																																								
Day of Week																																								
Time																																								

Basal Body Temperature (°F) — °C scale: 37.9, 37.8, 37.7, 37.6, 37.5, 37.4, 37.3, 37.2, 37.1, 37.0, 36.9, 36.8, 36.7, 36.6, 36.5, 36.4, 36.3, 36.2, 36.1, 36.0, 35.9

Temperature rows (°F): 99, 9, 8, 7, 6, 5, 4, 3, 2, 1, 98, 9, 8, 7, 6, 5, 4, 3, 2, 1, 97

Fertility																																								
Menstruation																																								
Mucus																																								
Sensation																																								
Cervix																																								
Intercourse																																								

Notes:

Example:

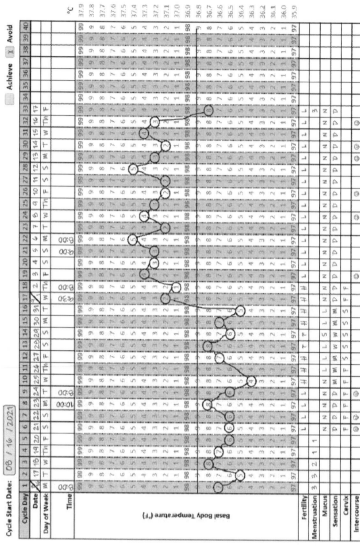

Key

Fertility:	Menstruation:	Mucus:	Sensation:	Cervix:
L = Low	1 = Light	N = Nothing	D = Dry	F = Firm
H = High	2 = Moderate	L = Little	M = Moist	S = Soft
P = Peak	3 = Heavy	S = Sticky	W = Wet	

Sympto-Thermal Method NFP Chart

Cycle Start Date: ___ / ___ / ___

Achieve   Avoid

Cycle Day	1	2	3	4	5	6	7	8	9	10	11	12	13	14	15	16	17	18	19	20	21	22	23	24	25	26	27	28	29	30	31	32	33	34	35	36	37	38	39	40
Date																																								
Day of Week																																								
Time																																								

Basal Body Temperature (°F)

°C
37.9
37.8
37.7
37.6
37.5
37.4
37.3
37.2
37.1
37.0
36.9
36.8
36.7
36.6
36.5
36.4
36.3
36.2
36.1
36.0
35.9

Fertility																																								
Menstruation																																								
Mucus																																								
Sensation																																								
Cervix																																								
Intercourse																																								

Notes:

Example:

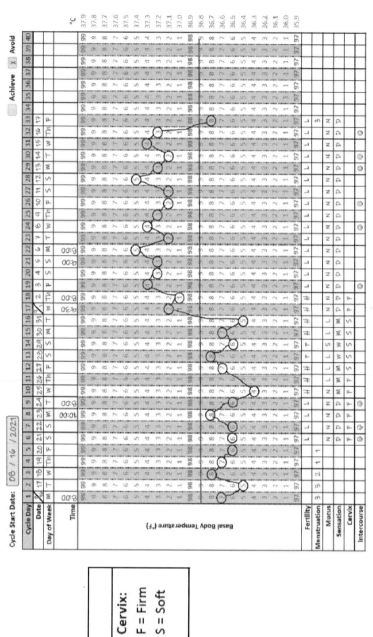

Key

Fertility:	Menstruation:	Mucus:	Sensation:	Cervix:
L = Low	1 = Light	N = Nothing	D = Dry	F = Firm
H = High	2 = Moderate	L = Little	M = Moist	S = Soft
P = Peak	3 = Heavy	S = Sticky	W = Wet	

Sympto-Thermal Method NFP Chart

Cycle Start Date: ___ / ___ / ___

Achieve ☐   Avoid ☐

Cycle Day	1	2	3	4	5	6	7	8	9	10	11	12	13	14	15	16	17	18	19	20	21	22	23	24	25	26	27	28	29	30	31	32	33	34	35	36	37	38	39	40
Date																																								
Day of Week																																								
Time																																								

Basal Body Temperature (°F) — with °C scale (37.9 down to 35.9)

Fertility																																								
Menstruation																																								
Mucus																																								
Sensation																																								
Cervix																																								
Intercourse																																								

Notes:

Example:

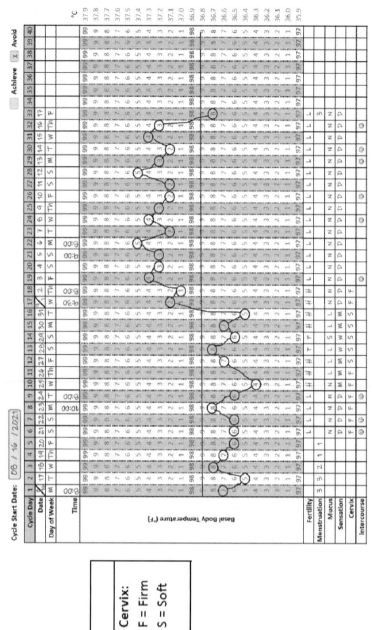

Key

Fertility:	Menstruation:	Mucus:	Sensation:	Cervix:
L = Low	1 = Light	N = Nothing	D = Dry	F = Firm
H = High	2 = Moderate	L = Little	M = Moist	S = Soft
P = Peak	3 = Heavy	S = Sticky	W = Wet	

Sympto-Thermal Method NFP Chart

Cycle Start Date: ___ / ___ / ___

Achieve ☐   Avoid ☐

Cycle Day	1	2	3	4	5	6	7	8	9	10	11	12	13	14	15	16	17	18	19	20	21	22	23	24	25	26	27	28	29	30	31	32	33	34	35	36	37	38	39	40	°C
Date																																									
Day of Week																																									
Time																																									
Basal Body Temperature (°F)																																									37.9
																																									37.8
																																									37.7
																																									37.6
																																									37.5
																																									37.4
																																									37.3
																																									37.2
																																									37.1
																																									37.0
																																									36.9
																																									36.8
																																									36.7
																																									36.6
																																									36.5
																																									36.4
																																									36.3
																																									36.2
																																									36.1
																																									36.0
																																									35.9
Fertility																																									
Menstruation																																									
Mucus																																									
Sensation																																									
Cervix																																									
Intercourse																																									

Notes:

Example:

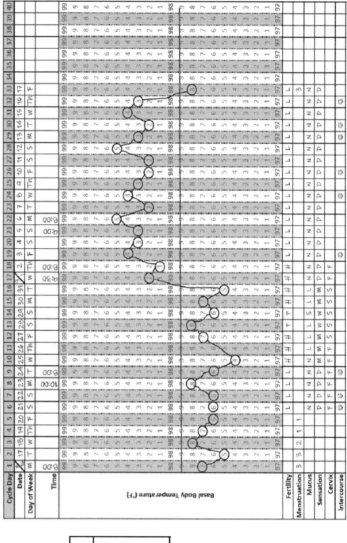

Cycle Start Date: 08 / 16 / 2021

Achieve ⬜ Avoid ⬛

Key

Fertility:	Menstruation:	Mucus:	Sensation:	Cervix:
L = Low	1 = Light	N = Nothing	D = Dry	F = Firm
H = High	2 = Moderate	L = Little	M = Moist	S = Soft
P = Peak	3 = Heavy	S = Sticky	W = Wet	

Sympto-Thermal Method NFP Chart

Cycle Start Date: ___ / ___ / ___

☐ Achieve ☐ Avoid

Cycle Day	1	2	3	4	5	6	7	8	9	10	11	12	13	14	15	16	17	18	19	20	21	22	23	24	25	26	27	28	29	30	31	32	33	34	35	36	37	38	39	40
Date																																								
Day of Week																																								
Time																																								

Basal Body Temperature (°F) — °C scale: 37.9, 37.8, 37.7, 37.6, 37.5, 37.4, 37.3, 37.2, 37.1, 37.0, 36.9, 36.8, 36.7, 36.6, 36.5, 36.4, 36.3, 36.2, 36.1, 36.0, 35.9

°F rows: 99, 9, 8, 7, 6, 5, 4, 3, 2, 1, 98, 9, 8, 7, 6, 5, 4, 3, 2, 1, 97

Fertility																																								
Menstruation																																								
Mucus																																								
Sensation																																								
Cervix																																								
Intercourse																																								

Notes:

Example:

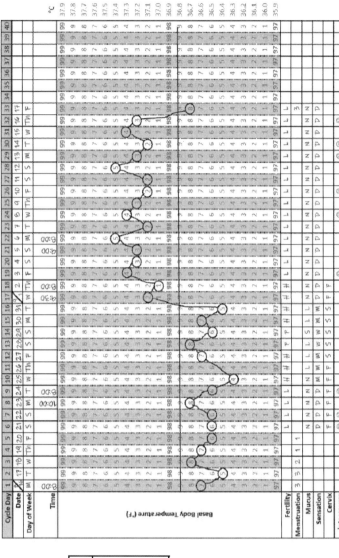

Key

Fertility:	Menstruation:	Mucus:	Sensation:	Cervix:
L = Low	1 = Light	N = Nothing	D = Dry	F = Firm
H = High	2 = Moderate	L = Little	M = Moist	S = Soft
P = Peak	3 = Heavy	S = Sticky	W = Wet	

Sympto-Thermal Method NFP Chart

Cycle Start Date: ___ / ___ / ___

Achieve ☐   Avoid ☐

Cycle Day	1	2	3	4	5	6	7	8	9	10	11	12	13	14	15	16	17	18	19	20	21	22	23	24	25	26	27	28	29	30	31	32	33	34	35	36	37	38	39	40
Date																																								
Day of Week																																								
Time																																								

Basal Body Temperature (°F)

Temperature scale (°C / °F):
37.9 = 99
37.8 = 9
37.7 = 8
37.6 = 7
37.5 = 6
37.4 = 5
37.3 = 4
37.2 = 3
37.1 = 2
37.0 = 1
36.9 = 98
36.8 = 9
36.7 = 8
36.6 = 7
36.5 = 6
36.4 = 5
36.3 = 4
36.2 = 3
36.1 = 2
36.0 = 1
35.9 = 97

Fertility	
Menstruation	
Mucus	
Sensation	
Cervix	
Intercourse	

Notes:

Example:

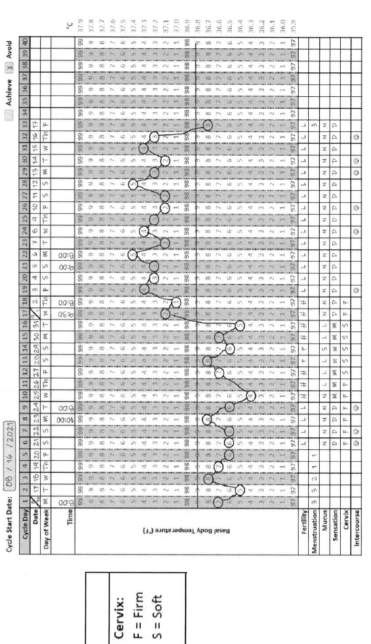

Key

Fertility:	Menstruation:	Mucus:	Sensation:	Cervix:
L = Low	1 = Light	N = Nothing	D = Dry	F = Firm
H = High	2 = Moderate	L = Little	M = Moist	S = Soft
P = Peak	3 = Heavy	S = Sticky	W = Wet	

Sympto-Thermal Method NFP Chart

Cycle Start Date: ___ / ___ / ___

Legend: ▢ Achieve   ▢ Avoid

Cycle Day	1	2	3	4	5	6	7	8	9	10	11	12	13	14	15	16	17	18	19	20	21	22	23	24	25	26	27	28	29	30	31	32	33	34	35	36	37	38	39	40
Date																																								
Day of Week																																								
Time																																								

Basal Body Temperature (°F) — °C scale:

37.9, 37.8, 37.7, 37.6, 37.5, 37.4, 37.3, 37.2, 37.1, 37.0, 36.9, 36.8, 36.7, 36.6, 36.5, 36.4, 36.3, 36.2, 36.1, 36.0, 35.9

(°F grid rows: 99, 9, 8, 7, 6, 5, 4, 3, 2, 1, 98, 9, 8, 7, 6, 5, 4, 3, 2, 1, 97)

	1	2	3	4	5	6	7	8	9	10	11	12	13	14	15	16	17	18	19	20	21	22	23	24	25	26	27	28	29	30	31	32	33	34	35	36	37	38	39	40
Fertility																																								
Menstruation																																								
Mucus																																								
Sensation																																								
Cervix																																								
Intercourse																																								

Notes:

Example:

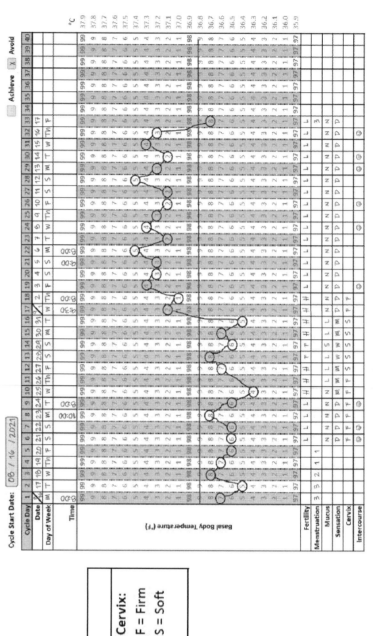

Key

Fertility:	Menstruation:	Mucus:	Sensation:	Cervix:
L = Low	1 = Light	N = Nothing	D = Dry	F = Firm
H = High	2 = Moderate	L = Little	M = Moist	S = Soft
P = Peak	3 = Heavy	S = Sticky	W = Wet	

Sympto-Thermal Method NFP Chart

Cycle Start Date: ___ / ___ / ___

Achieve ☐ Avoid ☐

	°C
99	37.9
9	37.8
8	37.7
7	37.6
6	37.5
5	37.4
4	37.3
3	37.2
2	37.1
1	37.0
98	36.9
9	36.8
8	36.7
7	36.6
6	36.5
5	36.4
4	36.3
3	36.2
2	36.1
1	36.0
97	35.9

Cycle Day: 1–40

Date

Day of Week

Time

Basal Body Temperature (°F)

Fertility

Menstruation

Mucus

Sensation

Cervix

Intercourse

Notes:

Example:

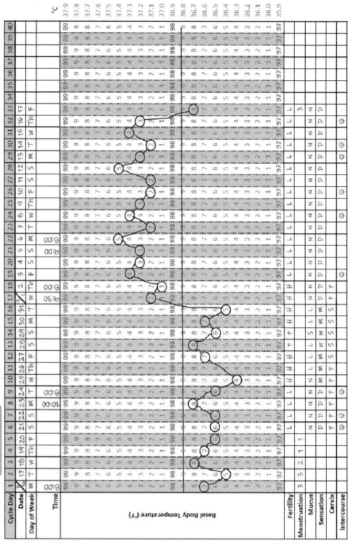

Cycle Start Date: 08 / 16 / 2021

Achieve ☒ Avoid

Key

Fertility:	Menstruation:	Mucus:	Sensation:	Cervix:
L = Low	1 = Light	N = Nothing	D = Dry	F = Firm
H = High	2 = Moderate	L = Little	M = Moist	S = Soft
P = Peak	3 = Heavy	S = Sticky	W = Wet	

Sympto-Thermal Method NFP Chart

Cycle Start Date: ___ / ___ / ___

☐ Achieve   ☐ Avoid

Cycle Day	1	2	3	4	5	6	7	8	9	10	11	12	13	14	15	16	17	18	19	20	21	22	23	24	25	26	27	28	29	30	31	32	33	34	35	36	37	38	39	40
Date																																								
Day of Week																																								
Time																																								

Basal Body Temperature (°F) — °C scale: 37.9, 37.8, 37.7, 37.6, 37.5, 37.4, 37.3, 37.2, 37.1, 37.0, 36.9, 36.8, 36.7, 36.6, 36.5, 36.4, 36.3, 36.2, 36.1, 36.0, 35.9

(°F grid marked 99 / 9 / 8 / 7 / 6 / 5 / 4 / 3 / 2 / 1 / 98 / 9 / 8 / 7 / 6 / 5 / 4 / 3 / 2 / 1 / 97 for each cycle day)

Fertility	
Menstruation	
Mucus	
Sensation	
Cervix	
Intercourse	

Notes:

Example:

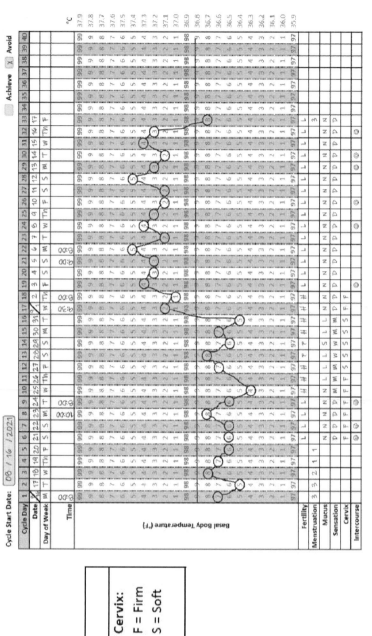

Key

Fertility:	Menstruation:	Mucus:	Sensation:	Cervix:
L = Low	1 = Light	N = Nothing	D = Dry	F = Firm
H = High	2 = Moderate	L = Little	M = Moist	S = Soft
P = Peak	3 = Heavy	S = Sticky	W = Wet	

Sympto-Thermal Method NFP Chart

Cycle Start Date: ___ / ___ / ___

Achieve ☐ Avoid ☐

Cycle Day	1	2	3	4	5	6	7	8	9	10	11	12	13	14	15	16	17	18	19	20	21	22	23	24	25	26	27	28	29	30	31	32	33	34	35	36	37	38	39	40	°C
Date																																									
Day of Week																																									
Time																																									

Basal Body Temperature (°F)

Temperature scale (°F / °C):
99 / 37.9, 9 / 37.8, 8 / 37.7, 7 / 37.6, 6 / 37.5, 5 / 37.4, 4 / 37.3, 3 / 37.2, 2 / 37.1, 1 / 37.0, 98 / 36.9, 9 / 36.8, 8 / 36.7, 7 / 36.6, 6 / 36.5, 5 / 36.4, 4 / 36.3, 3 / 36.2, 2 / 36.1, 1 / 36.0, 97 / 35.9

Fertility																																									
Menstruation																																								
Mucus																																								
Sensation																																								
Cervix																																								
Intercourse																																								

Notes:

Example:

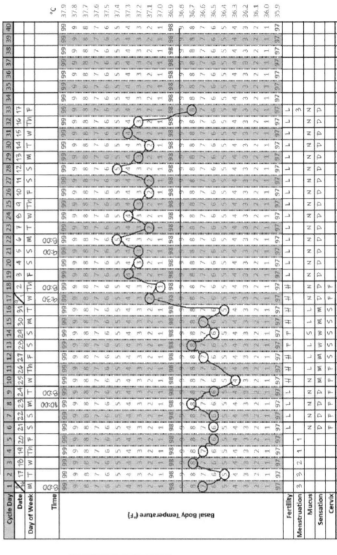

Key

Fertility:	Menstruation:	Mucus:	Sensation:	Cervix:
L = Low	1 = Light	N = Nothing	D = Dry	F = Firm
H = High	2 = Moderate	L = Little	M = Moist	S = Soft
P = Peak	3 = Heavy	S = Sticky	W = Wet	

Sympto-Thermal Method NFP Chart

Cycle Start Date: ___ / ___ / ___

Achieve ☐ Avoid ☐

Cycle Day	1	2	3	4	5	6	7	8	9	10	11	12	13	14	15	16	17	18	19	20	21	22	23	24	25	26	27	28	29	30	31	32	33	34	35	36	37	38	39	40	°C
Date																																									
Day of Week																																									
Time																																									

Basal Body Temperature (°F)

Temperature scale (°F / °C):
99 9 / 37.9, 99 8 / 37.8, 99 7 / 37.7, 99 6 / 37.6, 99 5 / 37.5, 99 4 / 37.4, 99 3 / 37.3, 99 2 / 37.2, 99 1 / 37.1, 99 0 / 37.0, 98 9 / 36.9, 98 8 / 36.8, 98 7 / 36.7, 98 6 / 36.6, 98 5 / 36.5, 98 4 / 36.4, 98 3 / 36.3, 98 2 / 36.2, 98 1 / 36.1, 98 0 / 36.0, 97 9 / 35.9

Fertility																																									
Menstruation																																									
Mucus																																									
Sensation																																									
Cervix																																									
Intercourse																																									

Notes:

Example:

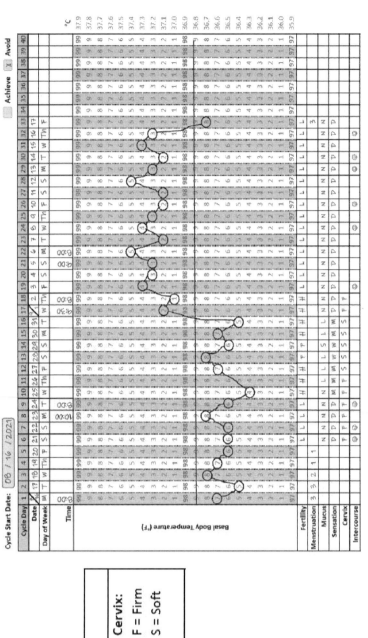

Key

Fertility:	Menstruation:	Mucus:	Sensation:	Cervix:
L = Low	1 = Light	N = Nothing	D = Dry	F = Firm
H = High	2 = Moderate	L = Little	M = Moist	S = Soft
P = Peak	3 = Heavy	S = Sticky	W = Wet	

Sympto-Thermal Method NFP Chart

Cycle Start Date: ___ / ___ / ___

Achieve ▢   Avoid ▢

Cycle Day	1	2	3	4	5	6	7	8	9	10	11	12	13	14	15	16	17	18	19	20	21	22	23	24	25	26	27	28	29	30	31	32	33	34	35	36	37	38	39	40	°C
Date																																									
Day of Week																																									
Time																																									

Basal Body Temperature (°F) — rows from 99.9 (37.9 °C) down to 97 (35.9 °C)

Fertility																																								
Menstruation																																								
Mucus																																								
Sensation																																								
Cervix																																								
Intercourse																																								

Notes:

Example:

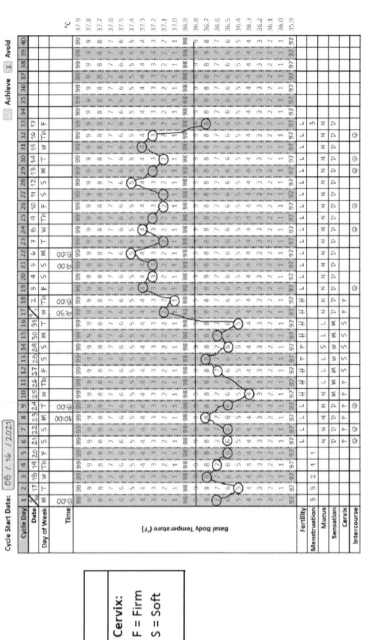

Key

Fertility:	Menstruation:	Mucus:	Sensation:	Cervix:
L = Low	1 = Light	N = Nothing	D = Dry	F = Firm
H = High	2 = Moderate	L = Little	M = Moist	S = Soft
P = Peak	3 = Heavy	S = Sticky	W = Wet	

Sympto-Thermal Method NFP Chart

Cycle Start Date: ___ / ___ / ___

Achieve ☐ Avoid ☐

Cycle Day	1	2	3	4	5	6	7	8	9	10	11	12	13	14	15	16	17	18	19	20	21	22	23	24	25	26	27	28	29	30	31	32	33	34	35	36	37	38	39	40
Date																																								
Day of Week																																								
Time																																								

Basal Body Temperature (°F) / °C scale:

37.9 (99), 37.8 (9), 37.7 (8), 37.6 (7), 37.5 (6), 37.4 (5), 37.3 (4), 37.2 (3), 37.1 (2), 37.0 (1), 36.9 (98), 36.8 (9), 36.7 (8), 36.6 (7), 36.5 (6), 36.4 (5), 36.3 (4), 36.2 (3), 36.1 (2), 36.0 (1), 35.9 (97)

	Fertility
	Menstruation
	Mucus
	Sensation
	Cervix
	Intercourse

Notes:

Example:

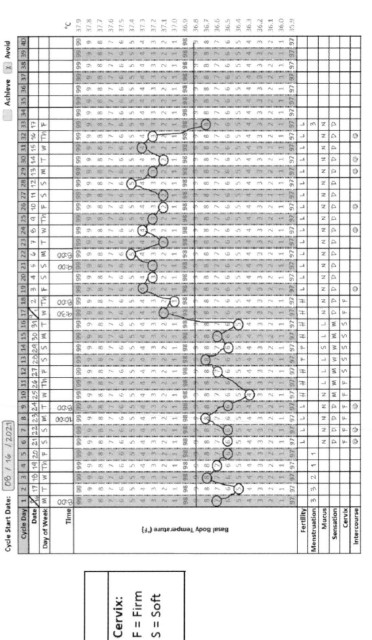

Key

Fertility:	Menstruation:	Mucus:	Sensation:	Cervix:
L = Low	1 = Light	N = Nothing	D = Dry	F = Firm
H = High	2 = Moderate	L = Little	M = Moist	S = Soft
P = Peak	3 = Heavy	S = Sticky	W = Wet	

Sympto-Thermal Method NFP Chart

Cycle Start Date: ___ / ___ / ___

Achieve ☐   Avoid ☐

Cycle Day	1	2	3	4	5	6	7	8	9	10	11	12	13	14	15	16	17	18	19	20	21	22	23	24	25	26	27	28	29	30	31	32	33	34	35	36	37	38	39	40
Date																																								
Day of Week																																								
Time																																								

Basal Body Temperature (°F) / °C

37.9 = 99, 37.8 = 9, 37.7 = 8, 37.6 = 7, 37.5 = 6, 37.4 = 5, 37.3 = 4, 37.2 = 3, 37.1 = 2, 37.0 = 1, 36.9 = 98, 36.8 = 9, 36.7 = 8, 36.6 = 7, 36.5 = 6, 36.4 = 5, 36.3 = 4, 36.2 = 3, 36.1 = 2, 36.0 = 1, 35.9 = 97

Fertility																																								
Menstruation																																								
Mucus																																								
Sensation																																								
Cervix																																								
Intercourse																																								

Notes:

Example:

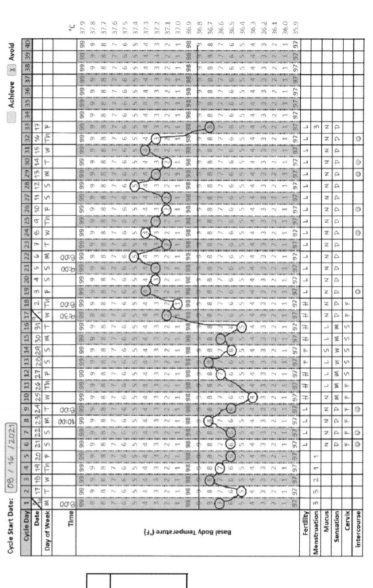

Key

Fertility:	Menstruation:	Mucus:	Sensation:	Cervix:
L = Low	1 = Light	N = Nothing	D = Dry	F = Firm
H = High	2 = Moderate	L = Little	M = Moist	S = Soft
P = Peak	3 = Heavy	S = Sticky	W = Wet	

Sympto-Thermal Method NFP Chart

Cycle Start Date: ___ / ___ / ___

☐ Achieve   ☐ Avoid

Cycle Day	1	2	3	4	5	6	7	8	9	10	11	12	13	14	15	16	17	18	19	20	21	22	23	24	25	26	27	28	29	30	31	32	33	34	35	36	37	38	39	40
Date																																								
Day of Week																																								
Time																																								

Basal Body Temperature (°F) — °C scale: 37.9, 37.8, 37.7, 37.6, 37.5, 37.4, 37.3, 37.2, 37.1, 37.0, 36.9, 36.8, 36.7, 36.6, 36.5, 36.4, 36.3, 36.2, 36.1, 36.0, 35.9

°F grid values per row: 99, 9, 8, 7, 6, 5, 4, 3, 2, 1, 98, 9, 8, 7, 6, 5, 4, 3, 2, 1, 97

Fertility	
Menstruation	
Mucus	
Sensation	
Cervix	
Intercourse	

Notes:

Example:

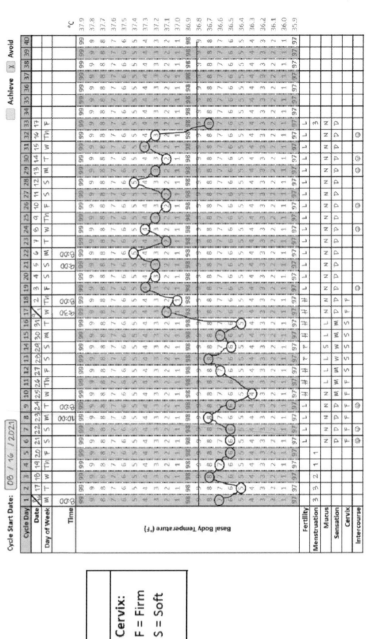

Key

Fertility:	Menstruation:	Mucus:	Sensation:	Cervix:
L = Low	1 = Light	N = Nothing	D = Dry	F = Firm
H = High	2 = Moderate	L = Little	M = Moist	S = Soft
P = Peak	3 = Heavy	S = Sticky	W = Wet	

Sympto-Thermal Method NFP Chart

Cycle Start Date: ____ / ____ / ____

Achieve ☐   Avoid ☐

Cycle Day	1	2	3	4	5	6	7	8	9	10	11	12	13	14	15	16	17	18	19	20	21	22	23	24	25	26	27	28	29	30	31	32	33	34	35	36	37	38	39	40
Date																																								
Day of Week																																								
Time																																								

Basal Body Temperature (°F) — with °C reference scale:
37.9, 37.8, 37.7, 37.6, 37.5, 37.4, 37.3, 37.2, 37.1, 37.0, 36.9, 36.8, 36.7, 36.6, 36.5, 36.4, 36.3, 36.2, 36.1, 36.0, 35.9

Temperature gridlines (°F): 99, 9, 8, 7, 6, 5, 4, 3, 2, 1, 98, 9, 8, 7, 6, 5, 4, 3, 2, 1, 97

Fertility																																								
Menstruation																																								
Mucus																																								
Sensation																																								
Cervix																																								
Intercourse																																								

Notes:

Example:

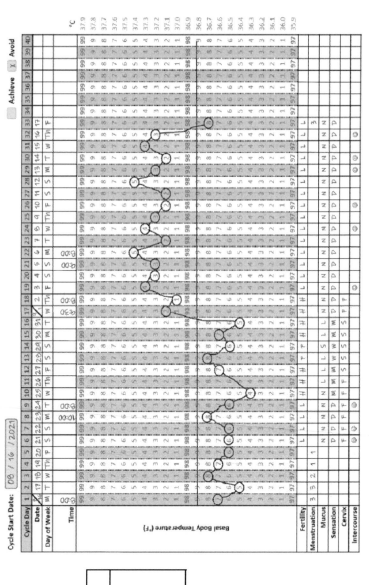

Key

Menstruation:	Mucus:	Sensation:	Cervix:
1 = Light	N = Nothing	D = Dry	F = Firm
2 = Moderate	L = Little	M = Moist	S = Soft
3 = Heavy	S = Sticky	W = Wet	

Fertility:

L = Low

H = High

P = Peak

Sympto-Thermal Method NFP Chart

Cycle Start Date: ___ / ___ / ___

☐ Achieve ☐ Avoid

Cycle Day	1	2	3	4	5	6	7	8	9	10	11	12	13	14	15	16	17	18	19	20	21	22	23	24	25	26	27	28	29	30	31	32	33	34	35	36	37	38	39	40	°C
Date																																									
Day of Week																																									
Time																																									

Basal Body Temperature (°F) — temperature scale rows from 99.9 down to 97 (°F), corresponding to 37.9 down to 35.9 °C

Fertility																																									
Menstruation																																									
Mucus																																									
Sensation																																									
Cervix																																									
Intercourse																																									

Notes:

Example:

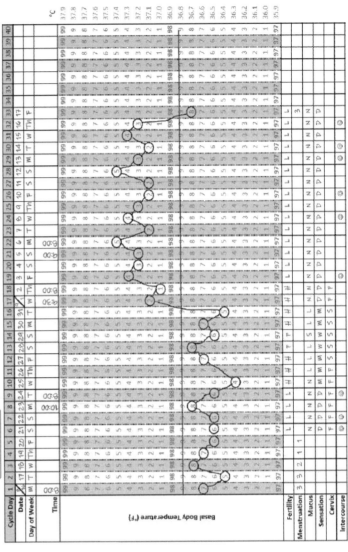

Key

Fertility:	Menstruation:	Mucus:	Sensation:	Cervix:
L = Low	1 = Light	N = Nothing	D = Dry	F = Firm
H = High	2 = Moderate	L = Little	M = Moist	S = Soft
P = Peak	3 = Heavy	S = Sticky	W = Wet	

Sympto-Thermal Method NFP Chart

Cycle Start Date: ___ / ___ / ___

Achieve ☐   Avoid ☐

Cycle Day	1	2	3	4	5	6	7	8	9	10	11	12	13	14	15	16	17	18	19	20	21	22	23	24	25	26	27	28	29	30	31	32	33	34	35	36	37	38	39	40	°C
Date																																									
Day of Week																																									
Time																																									

Basal Body Temperature (°F) — rows from 99.9 (37.9°C) down to 97 (35.9°C)

Fertility	
Menstruation	
Mucus	
Sensation	
Cervix	
Intercourse	

Notes:

Example:

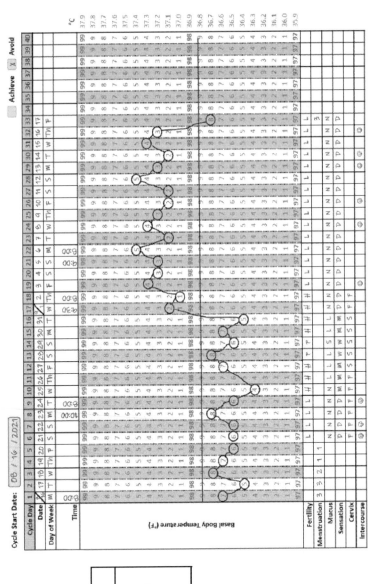

Key

Fertility:	Menstruation:	Mucus:	Sensation:	Cervix:
L = Low	1 = Light	N = Nothing	D = Dry	F = Firm
H = High	2 = Moderate	L = Little	M = Moist	S = Soft
P = Peak	3 = Heavy	S = Sticky	W = Wet	

Sympto-Thermal Method NFP Chart

Cycle Start Date: ___ / ___ / ___

Achieve ☐   Avoid ☐

Cycle Day	1	2	3	4	5	6	7	8	9	10	...	40
Date												
Day of Week												
Time												
Basal Body Temperature (°F)												
Fertility												
Menstruation												
Mucus												
Sensation												
Cervix												
Intercourse												

°C scale (Basal Body Temperature):
37.9, 37.8, 37.7, 37.6, 37.5, 37.4, 37.3, 37.2, 37.1, 37.0, 36.9, 36.8, 36.7, 36.6, 36.5, 36.4, 36.3, 36.2, 36.1, 36.0, 35.9

Notes:

Example:

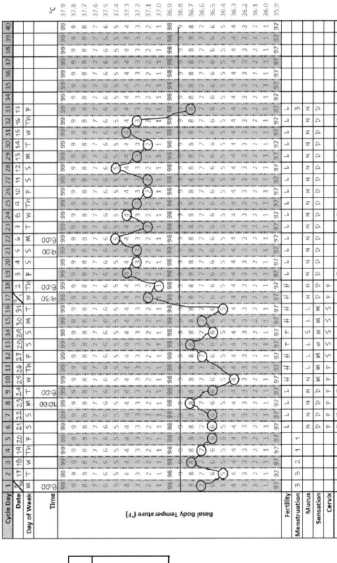

Key

Fertility:	Menstruation:	Mucus:	Sensation:	Cervix:
L = Low	1 = Light	N = Nothing	D = Dry	F = Firm
H = High	2 = Moderate	L = Little	M = Moist	S = Soft
P = Peak	3 = Heavy	S = Sticky	W = Wet	

Sympto-Thermal Method NFP Chart

Cycle Start Date: ___ / ___ / ___

Achieve ☐   Avoid ☐

Cycle Day	1	2	3	4	5	6	7	8	9	10	11	12	13	14	15	16	17	18	19	20	21	22	23	24	25	26	27	28	29	30	31	32	33	34	35	36	37	38	39	40	°C
Date																																									
Day of Week																																									
Time																																									

Basal Body Temperature (°F) — scale rows (99 … 97) with corresponding °C values: 37.9, 37.8, 37.7, 37.6, 37.5, 37.4, 37.3, 37.2, 37.1, 37.0, 36.9, 36.8, 36.7, 36.6, 36.5, 36.4, 36.3, 36.2, 36.1, 36.0, 35.9

Fertility	
Menstruation	
Mucus	
Sensation	
Cervix	
Intercourse	

Notes:

Example:

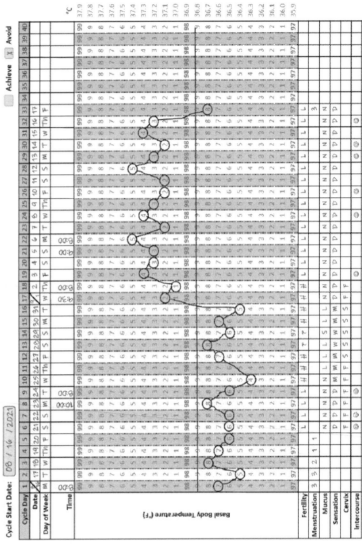

Key

Fertility:	Menstruation:	Mucus:	Sensation:	Cervix:
L = Low	1 = Light	N = Nothing	D = Dry	F = Firm
H = High	2 = Moderate	L = Little	M = Moist	S = Soft
P = Peak	3 = Heavy	S = Sticky	W = Wet	

Sympto-Thermal Method NFP Chart

Cycle Start Date: ____ / ____ / ____

Achieve ☐   Avoid ☐

Cycle Day	1	2	3	4	5	6	7	8	9	10	11	12	13	14	15	16	17	18	19	20	21	22	23	24	25	26	27	28	29	30	31	32	33	34	35	36	37	38	39	40	°C
Date																																									
Day of Week																																									
Time																																									

Basal Body Temperature (°F)

Temperature scale (°F / °C):
99 / 37.9, 9 / 37.8, 8 / 37.7, 7 / 37.6, 6 / 37.5, 5 / 37.4, 4 / 37.3, 3 / 37.2, 2 / 37.1, 1 / 37.0, 98 / 36.9, 9 / 36.8, 8 / 36.7, 7 / 36.6, 6 / 36.5, 5 / 36.4, 4 / 36.3, 3 / 36.2, 2 / 36.1, 1 / 36.0, 97 / 35.9

Fertility	
Menstruation	
Mucus	
Sensation	
Cervix	
Intercourse	

Notes:

Example:

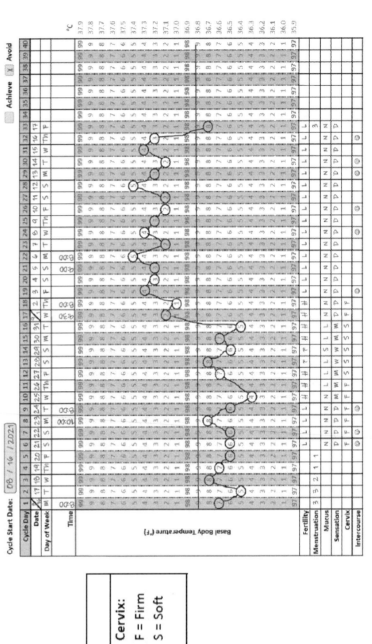

Key

Fertility:	Menstruation:	Mucus:	Sensation:	Cervix:
L = Low	1 = Light	N = Nothing	D = Dry	F = Firm
H = High	2 = Moderate	L = Little	M = Moist	S = Soft
P = Peak	3 = Heavy	S = Sticky	W = Wet	

Sympto-Thermal Method NFP Chart

Cycle Start Date: ___ / ___ / ___

Achieve ☐ Avoid ☐

Cycle Day	1	2	3	4	5	6	7	8	9	10	11	12	13	14	15	16	17	18	19	20	21	22	23	24	25	26	27	28	29	30	31	32	33	34	35	36	37	38	39	40
Date																																								
Day of Week																																								
Time																																								

Basal Body Temperature (°F) — scale (°C): 37.9, 37.8, 37.7, 37.6, 37.5, 37.4, 37.3, 37.2, 37.1, 37.0, 36.9, 36.8, 36.7, 36.6, 36.5, 36.4, 36.3, 36.2, 36.1, 36.0, 35.9

°F rows: 99, 9, 8, 7, 6, 5, 4, 3, 2, 1, 98, 9, 8, 7, 6, 5, 4, 3, 2, 1, 97

Fertility																																								
Menstruation																																								
Mucus																																								
Sensation																																								
Cervix																																								
Intercourse																																								

Notes:

Example:

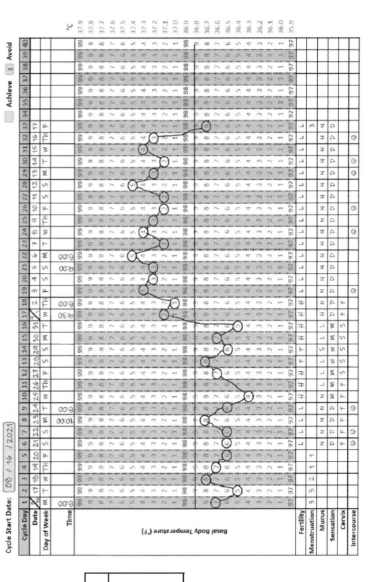

Key

Fertility:	Menstruation:	Mucus:	Sensation:	Cervix:
L = Low	1 = Light	N = Nothing	D = Dry	F = Firm
H = High	2 = Moderate	L = Little	M = Moist	S = Soft
P = Peak	3 = Heavy	S = Sticky	W = Wet	

Sympto-Thermal Method NFP Chart

Cycle Start Date: ___ / ___ / ___

☐ Achieve ☐ Avoid

Cycle Day	1	2	3	4	5	6	7	8	9	10	11	12	13	14	15	16	17	18	19	20	21	22	23	24	25	26	27	28	29	30	31	32	33	34	35	36	37	38	39	40
Date																																								
Day of Week																																								
Time																																								

Basal Body Temperature (°F)

Temperature scale (°C): 37.9, 37.8, 37.7, 37.6, 37.5, 37.4, 37.3, 37.2, 37.1, 37.0, 36.9, 36.8, 36.7, 36.6, 36.5, 36.4, 36.3, 36.2, 36.1, 36.0, 35.9

Temperature scale (°F): 99 / 9 / 8 / 7 / 6 / 5 / 4 / 3 / 2 / 1 / 98 / 9 / 8 / 7 / 6 / 5 / 4 / 3 / 2 / 1 / 97

Fertility																																								
Menstruation																																								
Mucus																																								
Sensation																																								
Cervix																																								
Intercourse																																								

Notes:

Example:

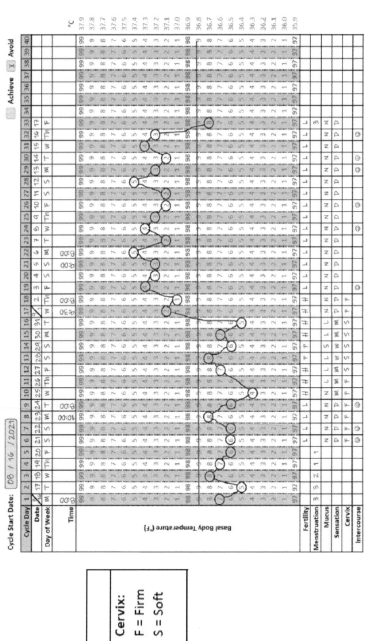

Key

Fertility:	Menstruation:	Mucus:	Sensation:	Cervix:
L = Low	1 = Light	N = Nothing	D = Dry	F = Firm
H = High	2 = Moderate	L = Little	M = Moist	S = Soft
P = Peak	3 = Heavy	S = Sticky	W = Wet	

Sympto-Thermal Method NFP Chart

Cycle Start Date: ___ / ___ / ___

Achieve ☐   Avoid ☐

Cycle Day	1	2	3	4	5	6	7	8	9	10	11	12	13	14	15	16	17	18	19	20	21	22	23	24	25	26	27	28	29	30	31	32	33	34	35	36	37	38	39	40	°C
Date																																									
Day of Week																																									
Time																																									

Basal Body Temperature (°F)

Temperature scale (°F / °C):
99 / 37.9, 9 / 37.8, 8 / 37.7, 7 / 37.6, 6 / 37.5, 5 / 37.4, 4 / 37.3, 3 / 37.2, 2 / 37.1, 1 / 37.0, 98 / 36.9, 9 / 36.8, 8 / 36.7, 7 / 36.6, 6 / 36.5, 5 / 36.4, 4 / 36.3, 3 / 36.2, 2 / 36.1, 1 / 36.0, 97 / 35.9

Fertility																																									
Menstruation																																									
Mucus																																									
Sensation																																									
Cervix																																									
Intercourse																																									

Notes:

Example:

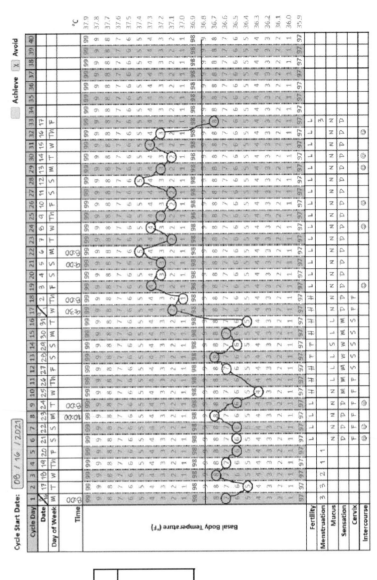

Key

Fertility:	Menstruation:	Mucus:	Sensation:	Cervix:
L = Low	1 = Light	N = Nothing	D = Dry	F = Firm
H = High	2 = Moderate	L = Little	M = Moist	S = Soft
P = Peak	3 = Heavy	S = Sticky	W = Wet	

Sympto-Thermal Method NFP Chart

Cycle Start Date: ___ / ___ / ___

Achieve ☐   Avoid ☐

Cycle Day	1	2	3	4	5	6	7	8	9	10	11	12	13	14	15	16	17	18	19	20	21	22	23	24	25	26	27	28	29	30	31	32	33	34	35	36	37	38	39	40	°C
Date																																									
Day of Week																																									
Time																																									

Basal Body Temperature (°F)

Temperature scale (°F: 99–97) with °C equivalents: 37.9, 37.8, 37.7, 37.6, 37.5, 37.4, 37.3, 37.2, 37.1, 37.0, 36.9, 36.8, 36.7, 36.6, 36.5, 36.4, 36.3, 36.2, 36.1, 36.0, 35.9

Fertility	
Menstruation	
Mucus	
Sensation	
Cervix	
Intercourse	

Notes:

Example:

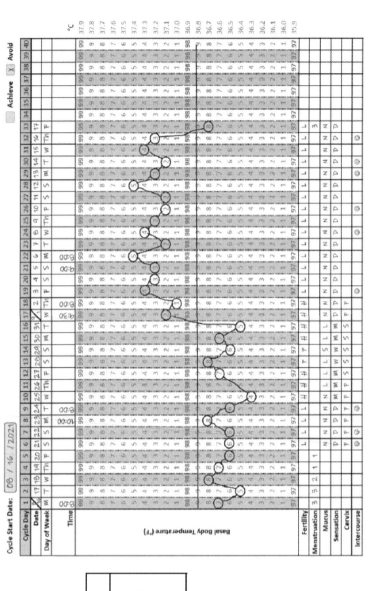

Key

Fertility:	Menstruation:	Mucus:	Sensation:	Cervix:
L = Low	1 = Light	N = Nothing	D = Dry	F = Firm
H = High	2 = Moderate	L = Little	M = Moist	S = Soft
P = Peak	3 = Heavy	S = Sticky	W = Wet	

Sympto-Thermal Method NFP Chart

Cycle Start Date: / /

Achieve ☐   Avoid ☐

Cycle Day	1	2	3	4	5	6	7	8	9	10	11	12	13	14	15	16	17	18	19	20	21	22	23	24	25	26	27	28	29	30	31	32	33	34	35	36	37	38	39	40
Date																																								
Day of Week																																								
Time																																								

Basal Body Temperature (°F) / °C scale: 37.9, 37.8, 37.7, 37.6, 37.5, 37.4, 37.3, 37.2, 37.1, 37.0, 36.9, 36.8, 36.7, 36.6, 36.5, 36.4, 36.3, 36.2, 36.1, 36.0, 35.9

Fertility																																								
Menstruation																																								
Mucus																																								
Sensation																																								
Cervix																																								
Intercourse																																								

Notes:

Example:

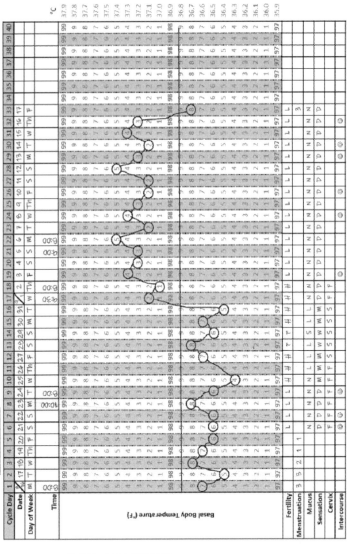

Key

	Menstruation:	Mucus:	Sensation:	Cervix:
Fertility:	1 = Light	N = Nothing	D = Dry	F = Firm
L = Low	2 = Moderate	L = Little	M = Moist	S = Soft
H = High	3 = Heavy	S = Sticky	W = Wet	
P = Peak				

Sympto-Thermal Method NFP Chart

Cycle Start Date: ___ / ___ / ___

Achieve ☐   Avoid ☐

Cycle Day	1	2	3	4	5	6	7	8	9	10	11	12	13	14	15	16	17	18	19	20	21	22	23	24	25	26	27	28	29	30	31	32	33	34	35	36	37	38	39	40	°C
Date																																									
Day of Week																																									
Time																																									

Basal Body Temperature (°F) — scale (°F / °C):

°F	°C
99.9	37.9
99.8	37.8
99.7	37.7
99.6	37.6
99.5	37.5
99.4	37.4
99.3	37.3
99.2	37.2
99.1	37.1
99.0	37.0
98.9	36.9
98.8	36.8
98.7	36.7
98.6	36.6
98.5	36.5
98.4	36.4
98.3	36.3
98.2	36.2
98.1	36.1
98.0	36.0
97.9	35.9

Fertility	
Menstruation	
Mucus	
Sensation	
Cervix	
Intercourse	

RESOURCE LIST

Couple To Couple League: www.ccli.org

Fertility Appreciation Collaborative to Teach the Science (FACTS): www.factsaboutfertility.org

Fertility Awareness Method of Birth Control: www.fertilityawarenessmethodofbirthcontrol.com/

Live The Love: www.livethelove.org

Sympto Pro Fertility Education: www.symptopro.org

SymptoTherm Foundation: www.symto.org

Taking Charge of Your Fertility: www.tcoyf.com

Made in the USA
Las Vegas, NV
14 January 2022

41389294R00070